FROM FLOATING EGGS TO COKE ERUPTIONS

AWESOME SCIENCE EXPERIMENTS FOR KIDS
CHILDREN'S SCIENCE EXPERIMENT BOOKS

BABY PROFESSOR
EDUCATION KIDS

Speedy Publishing LLC

40 E. Main St. #1156

Newark, DE 19711

www.speedypublishing.com

Copyright 2017

In this book, we're going to talk about some fun science experiments. So, let's get right to it!

Experiments are fun to do at home or at school. Always make sure that there's an adult supervising when you perform experiments. Protect your eyes with safety goggles and make sure you stand some distance away from experiments you expect to explode!

EXPERIMENT 1
FLOATING EGG FUN

THINGS YOU'LL NEED

- Two uncooked eggs

- Plain tap water

○ Salt, about 6 tablespoons

○ Two tall drinking glasses

GLASS OF WATER WITH EGG

STEPS TO TAKE

Step One: Take the first drinking glass and fill it almost full with tap water.

Step Two: Gently lower one of the eggs into that glass.

Step Three: Take the second drinking glass and fill it halfway with tap water.

Step Four: Stir 6 tablespoons of salt into the water in the second glass.

Step Five: Pour more plain tap water into the second glass until it's almost full. Be careful not to mix the plain water with the salty water.

Step Six: Lower the second egg into the second glass and observe the results.

SALT

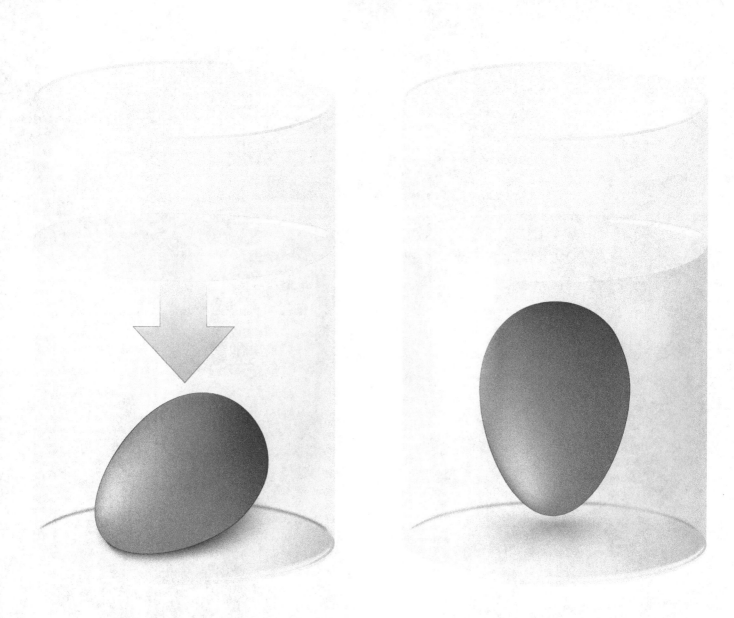

Fresh water

WHAT HAPPENED?

When you lowered an egg into the first glass, it went down to the bottom of the glass. However, in the second glass, the salt made the water in the bottom of the glass denser. It was dense enough for the egg to float! If you were very cautious not to disturb the salt water, your egg should be floating in the middle of the glass where the regular water and denser salt water meet.

Salt water

EXPERIMENT 2
COKE ERUPTION

THINGS YOU'LL NEED

- A sheet of wax paper
- A cutting board to place things on
- A knife

CUTTING BOARD AND KNIFE

- A roll of Mentos candy with at least 8 separate candies

- Two index cards and tape

MENTOS CANDY

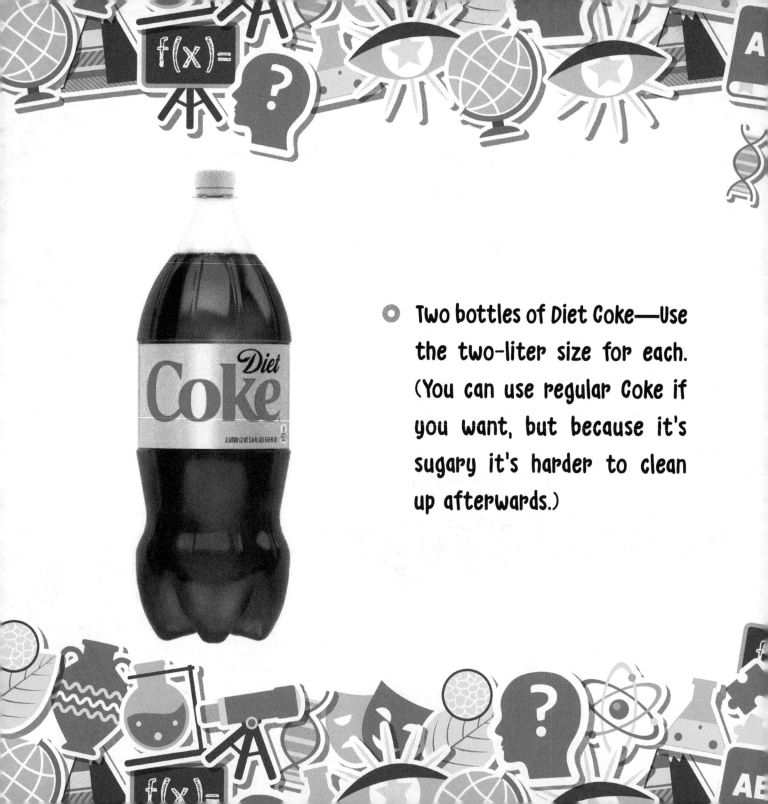

- Two bottles of Diet Coke—Use the two-liter size for each. (You can use regular Coke if you want, but because it's sugary it's harder to clean up afterwards.)

- An area outdoors that's a distance from buildings
- A flat surface like an outdoor table
- Safety goggles

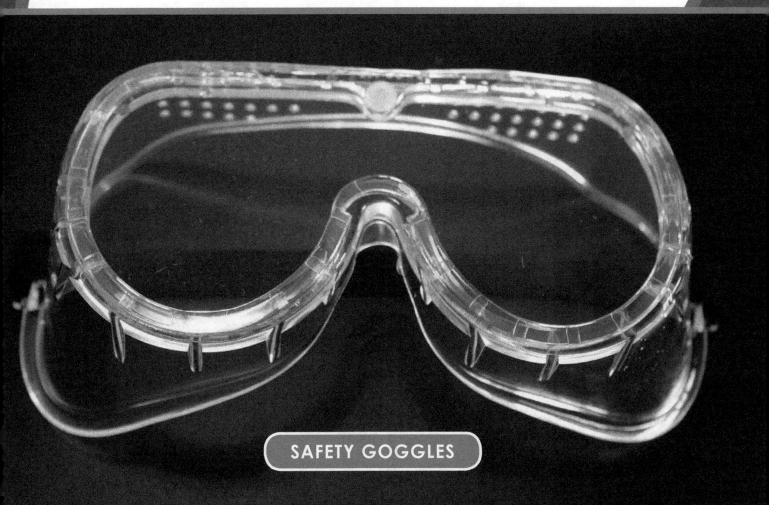

SAFETY GOGGLES

STEPS TO TAKE

Step One: Put a sheet of wax paper on top of the cutting board. Ask an adult to assist you and cut up and crush up four of the eight Mentos candies. Set them aside.

Step Two: Take one of the index cards and roll it up to make a tube. Use the tape to seal up the tube you've created. You need the tube to help you drop the candies into the Diet Coke bottles, so for the whole candies the diameter of the tube should be a little larger than the diameter of the candy so it will drop through easily.

Step Three: Make sure you wear safety goggles to protect your eyes and wear clothes you don't care about because they might get splashed!

Step Four: Place the first bottle of Diet Coke outdoors on a flat, stable surface. Make sure that you are away from all buildings or anything that could be hit by the resulting explosion.

Step Five: Take the cap off the bottle. Place the flat index card on top of the bottle opening.

Step Six: Line up your index tube with the bottle opening. Place the four whole candies in the tube. Pull the flat index card away quickly so the whole Mentos candies will drop into the bottle. Step away without knocking the bottle over.

Step Seven: Watch the resulting explosion and note how high it goes and how long it lasts.

Step Eight: Repeat the same steps with the second Diet Coke bottle and the crushed Mentos candies.

WHAT HAPPENED?

You may think that what you witnessed is a chemical reaction but instead it's a physical reaction. The Diet Coke is a carbonated soda. It's filled with a gas called carbon dioxide. The gas bonds with the water in the soda. While the soda is enclosed in the bottle, the gas stays in the solution because it's under pressure.

That's why when you pour some of the Coke into a glass it causes foam on the surface. The bubbles want to get out and escape!

COKE BUBBLES

To make even more bubbles, the bonds the carbon dioxide has with the water in the soda have to be disconnected. The Mentos candy looks smooth, but if you look at it under a microscope you'll see that it really has small bumps covering its surface. These bumps in the candy's surface help to break the bonds and make more bubbles, which causes the soda to erupt like a volcano! The faster the Mentos fall through the coke, the larger the eruption is. That's why the whole Mentos create a bigger, faster eruption than the crushed candies do.

EXPERIMENT 3
SWIMMING
GUMMY EELS

THINGS YOU'LL NEED

- Two clear drinking glasses

- A plastic fork

- A small dish to place your "worms"

- Four to six gummy worms

BAKING SODA

- 3 tablespoons of baking soda
- ½ cup of white vinegar
- 1 cup of water
- Kitchen shears

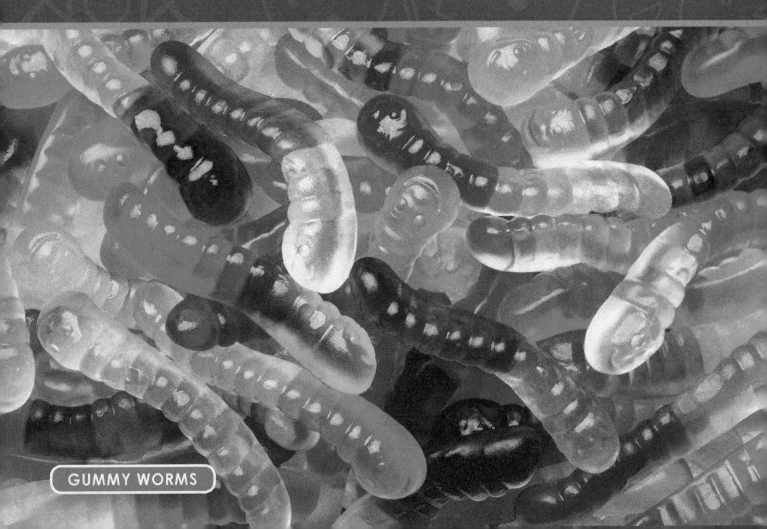

MIX WATER WITH BAKING SODA

STEPS TO TAKE

Step One: Using a kitchen shears, cut each candy worm lengthwise into at least four pieces. Get an adult to help you with this! You can also cut some smaller pieces too.

Step Two: In one of the glasses, combine the 1 cup of water with the 3 tablespoons of baking soda. Stir well.

Step Three: Add your candy worms to the combined mixture and let them "marinate" for about 15 minutes.

Step Four: Using a plastic fork, take the "worms" out of the mixture and place them in the small dish.

WATER WITH VINEGAR

Step Five: Place the ½ cup of vinegar into the second empty glass. Now, slowly put in the "worms" one at a time.

Step Six: You can do this experiment more than once by washing off your gummy worms and repeating the process. Eventually they'll dissolve, so you'll need more worms.

WHAT HAPPENED?

The chemical reaction of the baking soda and the vinegar causes your candy worms to become more like swimming eels. White vinegar is an acid and baking soda is a bicarbonate, which is a base. The combination of both causes a chemical reaction of an acid with a base. This reaction happens at the atomic level because the acid is poised to give away a proton and the base is poised to receive it. Their chemical reaction causes water, the gas carbon dioxide, and sodium acetate to form. The reaction happens quickly and that's why your gummy worms swim!

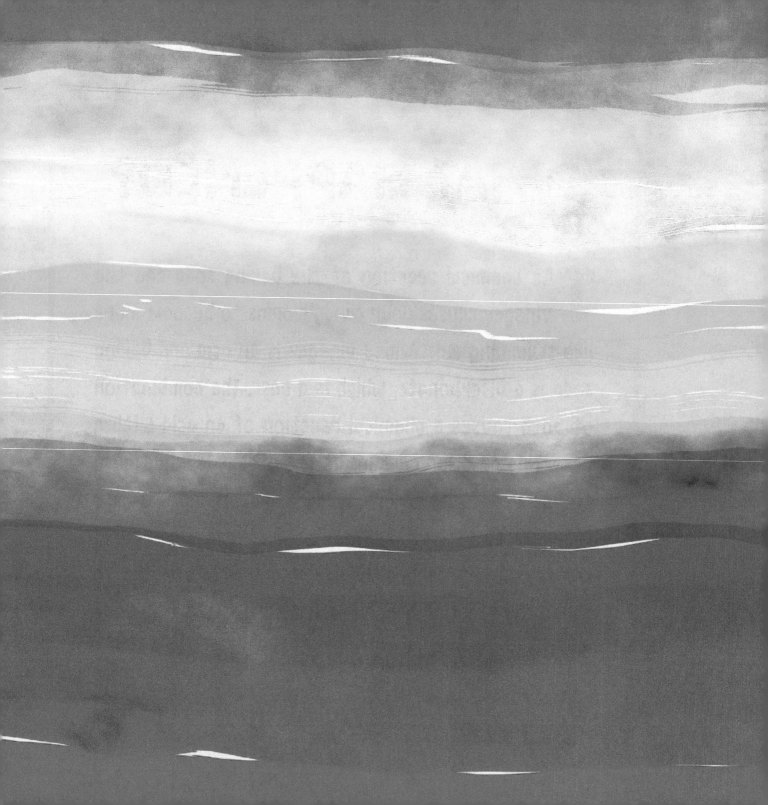

EXPERIMENT 4 RAINBOW-COLORED PAPER

THINGS YOU'LL NEED

- Clear nail polish
- Water
- A small bowl

NAIL POLISH

BOWL

- Small pieces of black paper
- Paper towels

PAPER TOWEL

BLACK PAPER

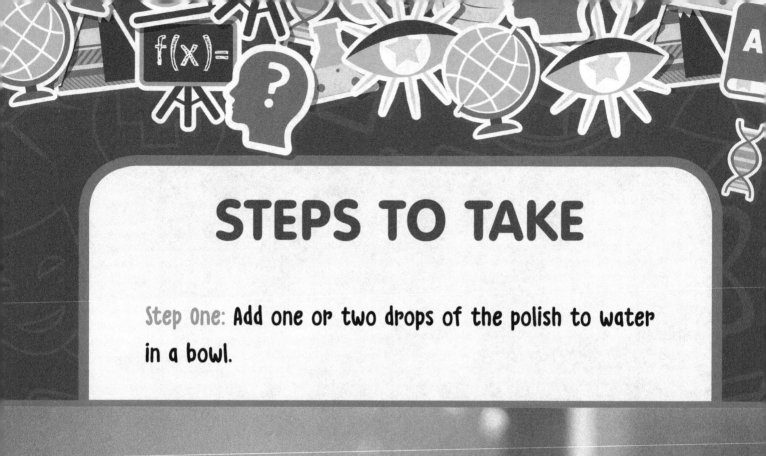

STEPS TO TAKE

Step One: Add one or two drops of the polish to water in a bowl.

Step Two: As soon as the polish spreads out over the water surface, dip each piece of paper very quickly into the water. Then, place each piece on a paper towel so it can dry out.

Step Three: As soon as the black paper is dry, which should just take a few minutes, angle it in different directions so you can see the varying rainbow patterns. To get the best view, hold the pieces next to a very sunny window.

BLACK PAPER WITH RAINBOW EFFECT

Step Four: You'll need to do the dipping quickly otherwise the nail polish will create a dry film over the water's surface. If that happens, scoop it out of the water and try to do the experiment again. Make sure to dip the paper in within 8-10 seconds of placing the polish in the water.

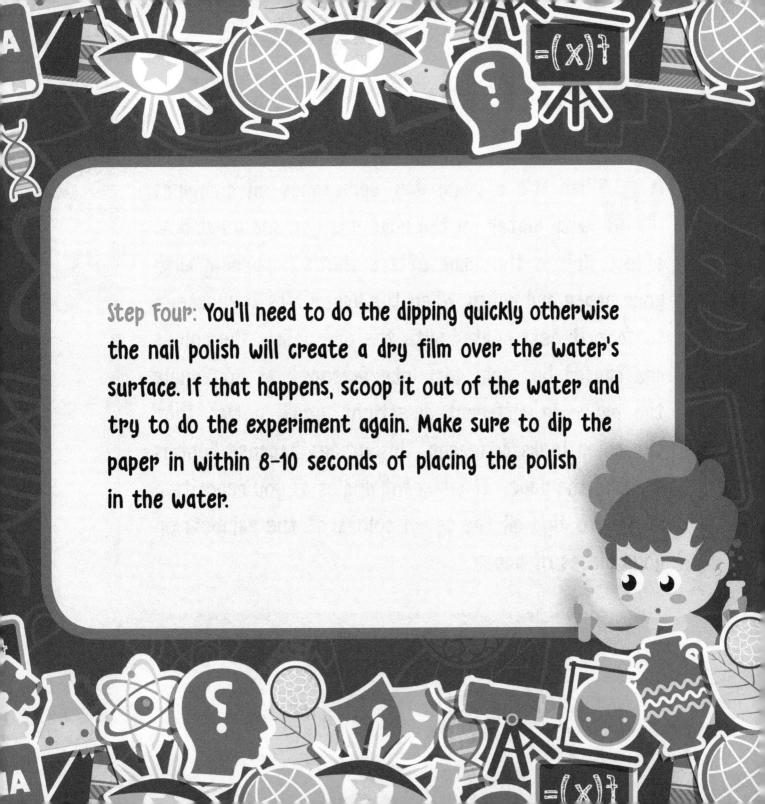

WHAT HAPPENED?

When it's a rainy day, sometimes oil combines with water on the road and you see a rainbow effect. This is the same effect that's happening with your paper and polish. When the paper hits the water's surface, it gets coated with the oily polish. The colors are caused by "thin film interference." As you angle the paper in different directions, you'll notice that the color looks different. This occurs because light is striking the paper at different angles as you reposition it. Try to find all the seven colors of the rainbow on your pieces of paper.

SUMMARY

There are so many fun experiments you can try at home or in school. Some experiments show chemical reactions and others show physical reactions. Make sure there is an adult supervising when you perform experiments and don't forget to make sure everyone wears safety goggles. Use a journal to write down what you think will happen before you begin the experiment. Did it turn out the way your hypothesis predicted it would? Why or why not? Summarize your conclusions. By using an experiment to test what you predict will happen, you're using the scientific method.

Awesome! Now that you've read about some fun science experiments you may want to read about some experiments with light in the Baby Professor book Light Surely Travels Fast! Science Book of Experiments.

Visit

BABY PROFESSOR
EDUCATION KIDS

www.BabyProfessorBooks.com

to download Free Baby Professor eBooks
and view our catalog of new and exciting
Children's Books

CPSIA information can be obtained
at www.ICGtesting.com
Printed in the USA
LVHW062201261119
638663LV00017B/907/P